HINA
The Goddess

HINA
The Goddess

written and illustrated by

Dietrich Varez

PETROGLYPH PRESS

Born on a stormy night full of intrigue and mystery, "Hina, The Goddess" has origins almost as wondrous as the tales of Hina herself.

While viewing performances of the powerful and ancient Kahiko form of hula at the 1986 Merrie Monarch Festival in Hilo, Hawai'i, the audience had an unforgettable experience. A raging storm swept over Hilo. Thunder clapped and lightning struck, plunging the entire town of Hilo, including the festival, into utter darkness.

Many wondered if it was mere coincidence that the evening's events included a compulsory chant for the wahine which spoke of Hina and the gourd calabash in which she captured three windstorms. Known for her forceful ways and power over the physical world, Hina is not to be taken lightly. One halau took this sign from the heavens so seriously that they withdrew from the competition.

Dietrich Varez was so struck by this incident and the power of the chant, he was inspired to create the first of the block prints appearing in "Hina, The Goddess" picturing Hina with her calabash. As his interest was piqued, he went on to delve further into the mythology of Hina in her many forms and from his research was inspired to create a series of block prints representing the many amazing and varied tales associated with Hina.

Petroglyph Press is proud to present this culmination of experience, imagination and talent so vividly portrayed in Varez's signature style block prints and corresponding legends. We believe you, too, will feel the presence of the goddess Hina as you experience "Hina, The Goddess" for yourself.

HINA, The Goddess
Copyright 2002 by Dietrich Varez
First Printing - March 2002; Second Printing - March 2003
New Petite Edition - April 2009

Published by the Petroglyph Press, Ltd.
books@petroglyphpress.com
www.PetroglyphPress.com ~ Facebook.com/PetroglyphHilo

ISBN 978-0-912180-66-3

-FOREWORD-

The name Hina, or variations thereof, occurs in mythologies throughout the Pacific. Hina usually refers to a strong female creative force as personified by a goddess over a specific domain. In Hawaiian mythology, for example, there is Hina-puku-iʻa (Hina-gathering-seafood) the goddess of fishermen. Or there is Hina-ʻopu-hala-koʻa who gave birth to all reef life. Another more popular Hina is the goddess of the moon.

There are many forms of Hina in Hawaiian myth and legend and the distinctions between them are not always clear. Any attempt to rigidly distinguish between all the individual Hina manifestations could surely be challenged. Furthermore, the indistinctions between the various Hina forms add a wonderful poetic ambiguity very characteristic of Hawaiian language and tradition.

This collection of Hina images is intended to stimulate new interest in the very powerful and pervasive mythology of the goddess and all her forms.

DIETRICH VAREZ 2002

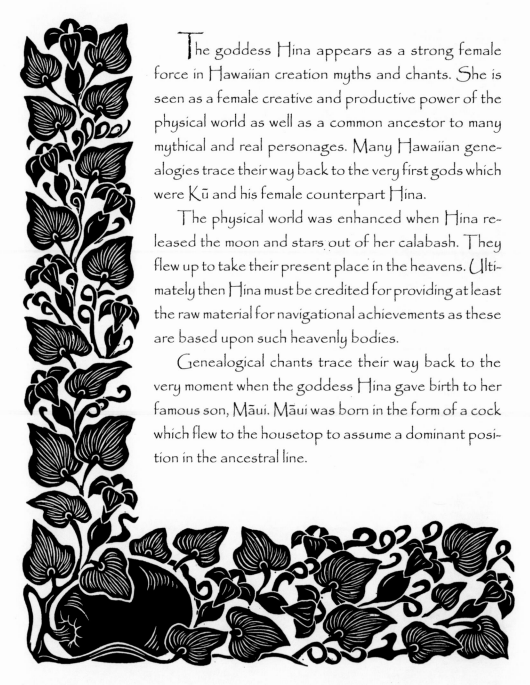

The goddess Hina appears as a strong female force in Hawaiian creation myths and chants. She is seen as a female creative and productive power of the physical world as well as a common ancestor to many mythical and real personages. Many Hawaiian genealogies trace their way back to the very first gods which were Kū and his female counterpart Hina.

The physical world was enhanced when Hina released the moon and stars out of her calabash. They flew up to take their present place in the heavens. Ultimately then Hina must be credited for providing at least the raw material for navigational achievements as these are based upon such heavenly bodies.

Genealogical chants trace their way back to the very moment when the goddess Hina gave birth to her famous son, Māui. Māui was born in the form of a cock which flew to the housetop to assume a dominant position in the ancestral line.

Moloka'i island is said to be the child of the goddess Hina, Moloka'i-a-Hina. Hina gave birth to the island after her short relationship with Wākea the primal father.

Another less flattering legend originates the island from an incestuous relationship between Wākea and his daughter Ho'ohoku-ka-lani.

For those interested in the origin and migratory routes of the Hawaiians it is of interest that there is a "Morotai" island in the Molucca Islands. Even more intriguing is the fact that the Moluccas were once called the "Sindas". Hina is called "Ina" or "Sina" in some parts of the Pacific. Early Spanish navigators in these spice islands spoke of an island named Morotoy de los Sindas which bears a tantalizing similarity to our own Moloka'i-a-Hina.

There is some belief that these linguistic similarities hint at a possible migratory trail from Hindustan to Hawai'i.

Another amazing birth attributed to the goddess Hina was that of the wondrous hog-child Kamapuaʻa.

Actually born as a pig Kamapuaʻa was a kupua, or shape-changer, and could assume the body of a hog, a handsome young man or even a fish.

Hinaʻs hog-child had many fantastic, comical as well as violent adventures. He was a notorious thief and relentless womanizer. His greatest conquest being the volcano goddess, Pele, with whom he had a tempestuous affair. Pele and Kamapuaʻa had a child and this grandson of Hina became the god of thieves and medical practitioners.

The collected adventures of Kamapuaʻa are an excellent example of a kaʻao, or lengthy story recited from memory. It is said that the Kaʻao of Kamapuaʻa took sixteen hours to recite. Such incredible feats of memory were common to old Hawaiian storytellers.

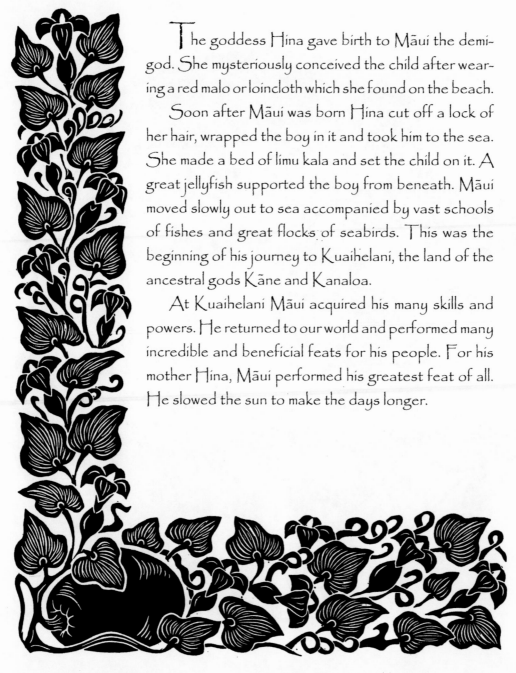

The goddess Hina gave birth to Māui the demigod. She mysteriously conceived the child after wearing a red malo or loincloth which she found on the beach.

Soon after Māui was born Hina cut off a lock of her hair, wrapped the boy in it and took him to the sea. She made a bed of limu kala and set the child on it. A great jellyfish supported the boy from beneath. Māui moved slowly out to sea accompanied by vast schools of fishes and great flocks of seabirds. This was the beginning of his journey to Kuaihelani, the land of the ancestral gods Kāne and Kanaloa.

At Kuaihelani Māui acquired his many skills and powers. He returned to our world and performed many incredible and beneficial feats for his people. For his mother Hina, Māui performed his greatest feat of all. He slowed the sun to make the days longer.

13

The boy, Palila, was born to Hina's daughter Mahinui. Palila was not an ordinary birth, he was born as a short piece of sennit cord. The puzzled parents tossed the curious cord onto their rubbish heap and left it there.

When Hina, the grandmother, came by to ask about her grandson Mahinui told her about the piece of cord. Hina went straight to the rubbish heap and searched until she found the length of cord. She hurried home with the cord and wrapped it in some clean white kapa. Hina wrapped this bundle three more times until it miraculously took the shape of a boy child. She named him Palila.

As grandmothers did in those days Palila was given careful attention. Hina built a special shelf for the child and fitted it with uluhe fern. Palila was fed nothing but bananas until he matured.

Under Hina's care and instruction Palila grew up to be a legendary adventurer and king of Hilo.

15

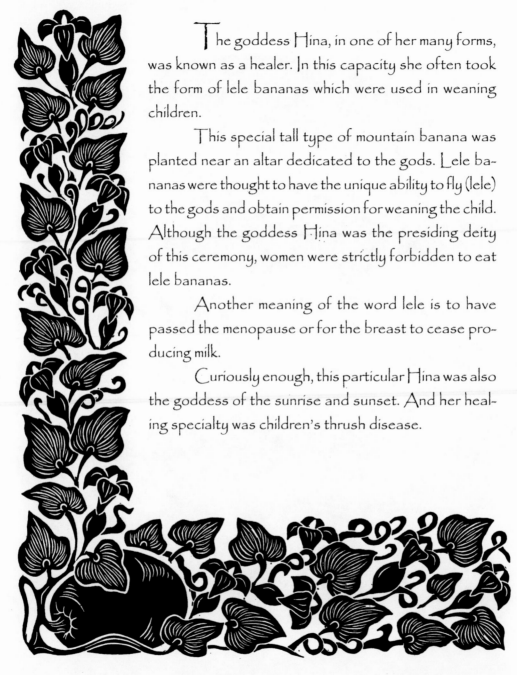

The goddess Hina, in one of her many forms, was known as a healer. In this capacity she often took the form of lele bananas which were used in weaning children.

This special tall type of mountain banana was planted near an altar dedicated to the gods. Lele bananas were thought to have the unique ability to fly (lele) to the gods and obtain permission for weaning the child. Although the goddess Hina was the presiding deity of this ceremony, women were strictly forbidden to eat lele bananas.

Another meaning of the word lele is to have passed the menopause or for the breast to cease producing milk.

Curiously enough, this particular Hina was also the goddess of the sunrise and sunset. And her healing specialty was children's thrush disease.

The goddess Hina, her husband Kuʻula and their son ʻAiʻai were the appointed fisherfolk for Kahoaliʻi the king of Hana, Maui.

One day the king sent his attendants to Hina's house to fetch some fresh fish. These attendants were jealous of Hina's household and returned to the king without fish. They invented lies and said Hina had insulted the king. Kahoaliʻi was furious and ordered his fisherfolk to be burned in their own home.

The warriors came and set the house on fire. Cleverly Hina placed three unripened gourds in the burning house. As the gourds exploded in the heat Hina and her family escaped.

Hina went to live in the sea with her husband Kuʻula. Their son went to live with a nearby friend. To avenge her family Hina caused all fish to disappear from Hana waters. Only when her son ʻAiʻai wove special fishtrap baskets according to her instructions did she fill his traps to overflowing. The fishermen of Hana, Maui have woven such traps or "hinaʻi" ever since.

18

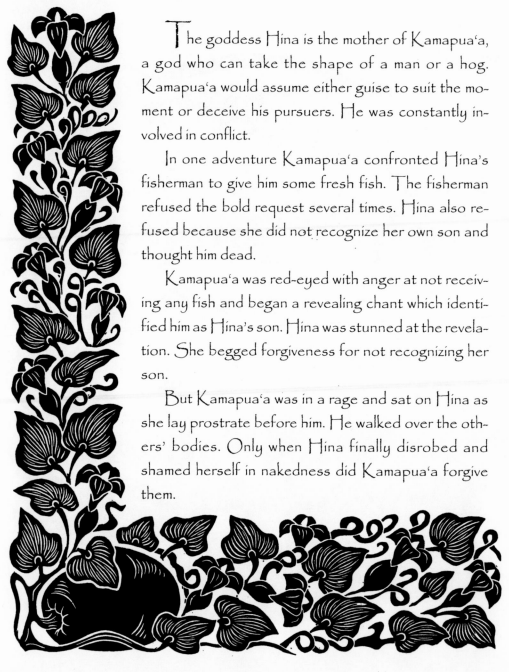

The goddess Hina is the mother of Kamapuaʻa, a god who can take the shape of a man or a hog. Kamapuaʻa would assume either guise to suit the moment or deceive his pursuers. He was constantly involved in conflict.

In one adventure Kamapuaʻa confronted Hina's fisherman to give him some fresh fish. The fisherman refused the bold request several times. Hina also refused because she did not recognize her own son and thought him dead.

Kamapuaʻa was red-eyed with anger at not receiving any fish and began a revealing chant which identified him as Hina's son. Hina was stunned at the revelation. She begged forgiveness for not recognizing her son.

But Kamapuaʻa was in a rage and sat on Hina as she lay prostrate before him. He walked over the others' bodies. Only when Hina finally disrobed and shamed herself in nakedness did Kamapuaʻa forgive them.

21

Hina is best known as goddess of the moon, or woman who worked in the moon. Her work was making the soft white kapa cloth which she did with unrivaled skill.

Hina goddess of the moon is perhaps the most widely known deity among the various island groups of the Pacific. There is even some speculation that Hina might derive her name from "Sin" moon god of ancient Assyria.

Hina did not always live in the moon. She once lived on earth but grew weary of her family and an overbearing husband. She fled up the rainbow to the sun but found it too hot there. Next she tried the moon and settled there in her legendary home.

Her very name, Hina, means white or silvery-gray in Hawaiian and suggests the color of pale moonlight.

23

There is a particular type of sweet potato named "hua-lani" meaning "seed of heaven". It is, however, a very earthly story familiar to all mothers that gives this plant its name.

The goddess Hina once gave birth to some imbecilic children who constantly made excrement. The disposal of excrement involved many strict rules and observances in Hawaiian society. Hina's husband insisted she laboriously follow all the unpleasant rules in disposing of the children's mess. Tired, weary and disgusted of it all Hina decided to abandon her household and flee to the serenity of the moon. Her panicked husband lunged up trying to stop her flight. He caught one of her legs but it broke off in his hands as Hina escaped.

The hau-lani sweet potato is named for that broken off piece of the fleeing Hina. Sweet potatoes are planted by pieces taken off from a mother plant.

25

It is well known that the goddess Hina was an expert at kapa making. So silky and soft was her cloth that we have never seen any like it.

But Hina did not always have an easy time with her clothmaking. The moist fibers had to be beaten together into sheets and then dried in the open sun. And in those early times, before Māui was born, the days were very short because the sun just raced across the sky and went down before anyone could get any work done. Hina never had enough time to make and dry her cloth with such a speedy sun.

The goddess grumbled to her son Māui about the sun speeding across the sky. The kapa cloth simply had not time nor warmth to dry.

Young Māui accepted the challenge of slowing the sun for his mother. He beat the blazing sun into submission and forced it to slow its present pace. A mother's boy this Māui.

27

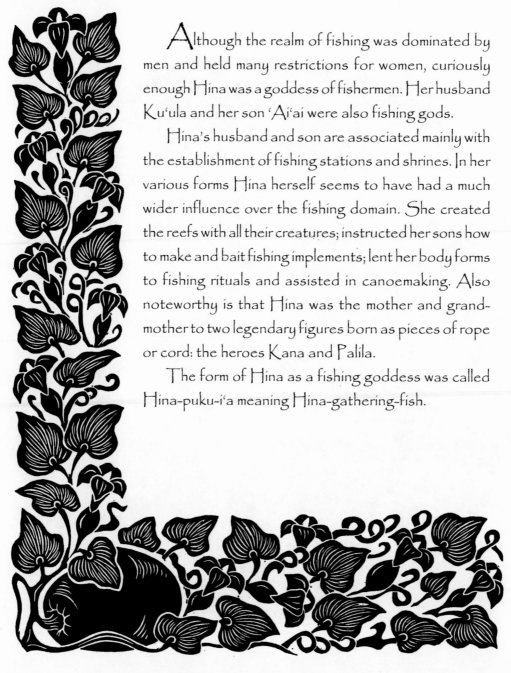

Although the realm of fishing was dominated by men and held many restrictions for women, curiously enough Hina was a goddess of fishermen. Her husband Ku'ula and her son 'Ai'ai were also fishing gods.

Hina's husband and son are associated mainly with the establishment of fishing stations and shrines. In her various forms Hina herself seems to have had a much wider influence over the fishing domain. She created the reefs with all their creatures; instructed her sons how to make and bait fishing implements; lent her body forms to fishing rituals and assisted in canoemaking. Also noteworthy is that Hina was the mother and grandmother to two legendary figures born as pieces of rope or cord: the heroes Kana and Palila.

The form of Hina as a fishing goddess was called Hina-puku-i'a meaning Hina-gathering-fish.

29

Another form of Hina was that of goddess of food plants. This Hina was called Hina-puku-ʻai or Hina-gathering-food. Sometimes this Hina was also called Hina-hele.

Hina-pukuʻai had a special calabash in which she kept food and food plants. She was lured away from her home by a chief and in the process spilled the contents of her calabash. These contents flew up to the heavens and became the moon and the stars.

It is no coincidence that Hina of the food plants should also be associated with the moon and stars. Hawaiians of old adhered to a strict lunar planting calendar for all their farming, and fishing as well. There are taro farmers to this day who will plant only at night and then give the new plants a particular tilt referred to as a "Hina".

A hula chant tells of a giant gourd calabash in which the goddess Hina kept three windstorms to release at will:

The Three Wind Storms of Hina

Hina's permanent residence lay at Kalua'aha
A cave dwelling hidden at Pa'o'iki Ridge
Protective eyes guard the Ko'olau districts
Wawahonua'aho, the great wind gourd
Sealed within are the three storms of Hina
Hina opens slightly the gourd cover
The Ilinahu wind gushes forth from Kamakou
Trees are uprooted and thrown over
In the path of the Ilinahu, shrubbery is twirled
Sweeping down and out to sea.
Hina opens halfway the gourd cover
Causing skies to darken on Pailolo Channel
Lightning flashes, thunder cracks, shaking the island
Wild gushes of wind causing ocean floods
Such is the way of the Uluhewa wind.
The worst storm is released, the Luluku
Crushed are the chiefs, crushed is the land
This is the way Moloka'i, the child, is protected
Great Moloka'i, child of the Goddess Hina.

A chant for the Three Winds of Moloka'i

33

Hina, goddess of corals, spiny sea creatures and mother of all reef-life provided the shells from which Māui the demigod made his famous fishhook. With this hook named Manai-a-ka-Iani (come-from-heaven) Māui fished the Hawaiian islands out of the sea.

Māui used an ʻalae bird, sacred to Hina, as bait for his legendary hook. The bird struggled as it sank to the depths. It came apart. Thus the islands came up separated and not all in one piece as a continent.

There is some mention of an actual immense fishhook called the "fishhook of Māui". King Kamehameha I supposedly owned it for a while. He failed at various attempts to break it. To his dismay a brother-in-law did manage finally to break the hook and it has not been seen since.

35

The utilitarian and ceremonial importance of bamboo in Hawaiian as well as many other cultures can hardly be overestimated. It is fitting therefore that the goddess Hina is credited with having brought bamboo to Hawai'i from Kahiki.

As told in the Kumulipo, Hawai'i's creation chant, Hina's son Māui performed his fourth great feat with the bamboo of Kane and Kanaloa. This association with the bamboo establishes Hina's son as a chief of very high rank.

But the most widespread use of the bamboo was reserved for Hina herself. Hina held dominion over the art of kapa making. Once made, this wonderful soft bark cloth was often printed with intricate designs. The process was basically a block printing technique and the blocks or stamps were made exclusively from bamboo. This unique block printing technique is found nowhere else in Polynesia.

37

The art of canoe making involved much ritual and ceremony and was the exclusive domain of men.

It was, however, the goddess Hina who presided over the ritual of selecting a proper tree and laying out the vessel itself.

When Hina assisted canoe makers she took the name of Lea and assumed the form of an 'elepaio bird. This bird has a voracious appetite for tree boring insects and flies. If the bird pecked on a tree canoe makers would know it to be fouled by insects or worms. They would not cut such a tree.

The positioning of the bow and stern of a canoe would also be determined by the habits of the bird. Where the 'elepaio first landed on the felled tree was to be the bow. Where the bird walked to thereafter would be the stern.

Many of the myths about the goddess, Hina involve references to gourds. Mostly these gourds have been fashioned into calabashes containing various and wondrous curiosities such as windstorms, heavenly bodies, and even common food plants.

One particular legend tells of the god Wākea, the primal father, on a fishing trip. He was far out at sea when a curious canoebailer floated by. This bailer had been made from a gourd, a common implement at that time. Wākea reached out and took the floating bailing gourd into his canoe. Miraculously the bailer changed into a beautiful girl named Hina.

Wākea took this Hina-of-the-bailer home and "warmed her by his fire." From their union all sorts of sea creatures were born. Again the gourd and Hina appear as strong symbols of procreation.

Some say the most beautiful Hina is the goddess associated with limu kala, a particular kind of seaweed used in medicine and ceremony. This very beautiful Hina goddess was said to live in the sea.

Limu kala, the seaweed sacred to Hina, was the central ingredient in the huikala ceremony for the purification of fishermen. The priest or kahuna would bring a bowl of water containing tumeric and limu kala amidst the fishermen sitting in a circle. A prayer of purification was called out.

A person suffering from physical or emotional illness was at times draped with a lei of limu kala. The patient would then enter the sea and as the lei began to float free the illness would drift away as well.

Limu kala is also associated with the small island of Molokini through an ancient legend.

43

Bathing in the bay of Hilo the goddess Hina noticed a curious new hill which she had not seen before. Hina put aside her surfboard and started up the lush green mound.

A gradual slope, but rather smooth and slippery, the hill was covered with all sorts of beautiful plants and flowers. Suddenly, just as Hina stood at the summit of the hill, it began to move. The hill moved swiftly out to sea and Hina was being carried away with it. She called out for help but no one was able to save her.

In truth the hill was actually a giant turtle. A great warrior chief had sent the turtle to abduct Hina and bring her to his home at Hāʻupu hill at Pelekunu on Molokaʻi.

Hina remained a captive at Hāʻupu hill until she was eventually rescued by the supernatural powers of her two sons, Kana and Niheu.

45

Wary as weary mothers might be concerning their son's doings, the goddess Hina, too, had a handful with her own young son, Māui.

Some soldiers had come by the young Māui's favorite fishing spot and taken him captive. Hina's pet guardian owl had witnessed the capture of the boy and reported it to Hina. The owl led Hina to the seaside temple where young Māui was bound for sacrifice the next morning.

Near the canoe landing by the temple Hina made her bed for the night. She caused the moon to appear and made the night so still and long that even the temple guards fell asleep. The owl flew silently in and cut the boys bonds.

Hina hid her son under a large flat rock as the morning came. She sat there innocently pretending to pick fleas out of her bedding as the guards searched for the missing boy.

47

In the classic archetypal tradition of the "damsel in distress" the goddess Hina was once held captive by a giant dragon-like lizard or mo'o named Kuna-loa in a cave in the Wailuku river near Hilo.

The captive Hina called out for help and her son Māui heard his mother's cries. He grabbed his legendary club and fearlessly sprang to the rescue.

Kuna, however, saw the eager youth approaching and quickly hid himself in a pool formed by the river. Māui heated huge stones in a fire and tossed them into the pools causing the water to boil. Kuna couldn't stand the steaming heat and came up to breathe. Just as his ugly head broke the surface of the water Māui's club came down. Kuna was dead and Māui had rescued his mother. A real mother's boy this Māui.

A long black rock formation in the Wailuku river remains to this day as the dead body of the giant mo'o, Kuna.

49

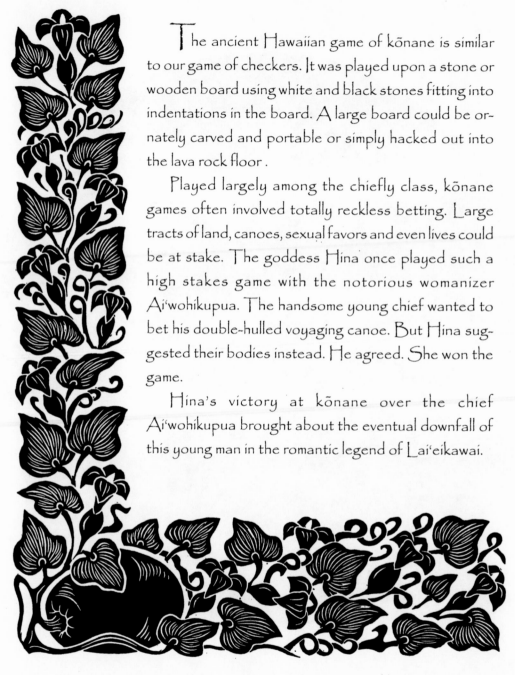

The ancient Hawaiian game of kōnane is similar to our game of checkers. It was played upon a stone or wooden board using white and black stones fitting into indentations in the board. A large board could be ornately carved and portable or simply hacked out into the lava rock floor.

Played largely among the chiefly class, kōnane games often involved totally reckless betting. Large tracts of land, canoes, sexual favors and even lives could be at stake. The goddess Hina once played such a high stakes game with the notorious womanizer Aiʻwohikupua. The handsome young chief wanted to bet his double-hulled voyaging canoe. But Hina suggested their bodies instead. He agreed. She won the game.

Hina's victory at kōnane over the chief Aiʻwohikupua brought about the eventual downfall of this young man in the romantic legend of Laiʻeikawai.

The Hālaʻi hills above the city of Hilo were always known for their rich soil, abundance of rain and lush crops. The goddess Hina was the chiefess here and her people wanted for nothing.

But once this paradise was beset by a drought which would not end. The plants all perished, the water ponds disappeared, and the hills turned to dry dust. Hina's people were starving in the fearsome famine.

Hina called her people together and had them dig a deep ground oven or imu. The goddess bid them build a huge imu to heat the oven stones. When the stones were shimmering with heat on the oven floor, Hina entered the pit and laid herself on the burning stones. The frightened people sealed the oven according to Hina's instructions.

For three days the oven remained sealed. Suddenly a spring of fresh water gushed forth nearby and Hina appeared in the steamy mist. When the imu was opened it was full of food and the famine was broken.

52

Puʻinokolu a Hina   Dietrich Varez

Above block print of Hina was inspired by the Merrie Monarch Festival of 1986.

Puʻinokolu a Hina

Kupene loloa a Hina i Kaluaʻaha
Peʻouʻou ke ana a Paʻoʻiki
Kiloliʻu maka pale Ke Koʻolau
Wawahonuaʻaho, he nui makani ipu
Uhipoʻi nei loko, Puʻinokolu a Hina
Hemo iki e Hina Ka uhipa
A mai Ke Ilinahu, e hakukoʻi i Kamakou
E ulaʻa, he laʻau e Kulaʻipohe pau
Ala hewa holo Ka Ilinahuʻe lau luehu
Hapupuʻe alo oke Kai
Hemo waho e Hina Ka uhipa
Hoʻoku mai Kumulani pauli maʻo Pailolo
A kauila, a hekili, lulu ka moku
E Oehu ahiu e hokaimoku
No leia ma Uluhewa
Hoʻuohi ka inoloa ika Luluku
E Kuʻi lili lani, e Kuʻi lili moku
Hela pale mau a Molokaʻi he kama
Molokaʻi nui a Hina

He mele no Puʻinokoluʻa Hina

The Three Wind Storms of Hina

Hina's permanent residence lay at Kaluaʻaha
A cave dwelling hidden at Paʻoʻiki Ridge
Protective eyes guard the Koʻolau districts
Wawahonuaʻaho, the great wind gourd
Sealed within are the three storms of Hina
Hina opens slightly the gourd cover
The Ilinahu wind gushes forth from Kamakou
Trees are uprooted and thrown over
In the path of the Ilinahu, shrubbery is twirled
Sweeping down and out to sea.
Hina opens halfway the gourd cover
Causing skies to darken on Pailolo Channel
Lightning flashes, thunder cracks, shaking the island
Wild gushes of wind causing ocean floods
Such is the way of the Uluhewa wind.
The worst storm is released, the Luluku
Crushed are the chiefs, crushed is the land
This is the way Molokaʻi, the child, is protected
Great Molokaʻi, child of the Goddess Hina.

A chant for the Three Winds of Molokaʻi

54

Dietrich Varez finds inspiration for his art from Hawaiian folklore and the natural beauty of the native ʻōhiʻa forest surrounding his home in Volcano, Hawaiʻi. His original prints are each individually created, hand-cut and produced by the artist himself in his own matchless style. A prolific and unconventional printmaker, Varez believes in making his art available to a broad, popular audience, by pricing his work so anyone can afford a hand printed, signed piece of art. Although he has had no formal art training, he has been creating his unique form of block prints since moving to Volcano and finding rich inspiration in the realm of Pele. Varez is further exploring his creativity with full color paintings in oil. His work is available at the Volcano Art Center, Honolulu Academy of Art, Bishop Museum and Kokeʻē Museum. Look for his signature artwork in the Reyn Spooner line of Hawaiian clothing. Visit www.DVarez.com for biographical information and a broad selection of Dietrich's work.

Dietrich Varez was born in Berlin, Germany in 1939. He has made his home in Hawaiʻi since the age of eight, when his mother, Ursula married Manuel Varez, an American soldier who adopted her two sons and brought the family home to Hawaiʻi. Growing up island style on Oʻahu, he attended the University of Hawaiʻi at Mānoa, earning a Masters degree in English. It was there he met his wife, Linda, a fellow artist, before moving the family to Hawaiʻi Island in 1968.

The creation:
The illustrations in "Hina, The Goddess" are created individually by the artist in the form of linoleum block prints. Each design is hand-cut from an original drawing which is transferred to the linoleum using carbon paper. Special cutting tools of three sizes are used to gouge out the image. Ink is then applied to the linoleum using a roller. The linoleum plate is inverted onto textured printmaking paper and rubbed uniformly. The paper is peeled from the plate surface and allowed to dry.

Books published by the Petroglyph Press